P9-CJJ-598

DALE CHIHULY
JAPAN 1990

DALE CHIHULY

JAPAN 1990

THE DELIGHTFUL THING ABOUT much new art of quality is its mischievous ability to break the rules. Dale Chihuly successfully resists being trapped in many of the pigeonholes that make for neat categories, but leech art of its complexity. First, he confidently bestrides the distinction between craft and art. And second, he has never felt the need to choose between abstraction and representation — between the natural and the invented.

There is in the United States a confusion as to the relative hierarchy implicit in the designations of art and craft. Artist and craftsman are categories for the ego, *not* ways in which to make useful or even meaningful esthetic distinctions. Chihuly occupies a rare position: His work is sometimes shown with crafts and sometimes with the work of painters and sculptors in art galleries. He is one of half a dozen members of his generation, workers in wood or clay or glass, whose work makes nonsense of these distinctions. Of course, this attempt to place Chihuly and his *objects de verre* in the context of American and international art is only of interest because of the stunning visual impact that the work evokes.

The first image that comes to mind when we attempt to describe Chihuly's work is one of fluid movement with elusively inflected highlights. Since my first encounter with Chihuly's work as the curator for twentieth-century art at the Metropolitan Museum of Art in New York in 1976, I have found it to be instantly memorable and of greater refinement with each viewing. Chihuly's work is strong and beautiful and, best of all, it is constantly evolving.

Chihuly has always been obsessed with the process of glass blowing. But his works are not merely records of their unique method of forming; they are an artist's dialogue with color and form. In his progression from the "Navajo Cylinders" to the "Venetians," his freedom in working with brilliant and fresh color juxtapositions and his play with the diaphanous clarities of glass show him updating art history through the unexplored medium of glass.

The other decorative device that Chihuly uses abundantly is the add-on, the collage element of glass melded to the formed vessel. The add-on is used with wit and daring, dramatic or comical, depending on the piece. they remind me of the way Matisse in his hotel room in Nice in the twenties and thirties kept a simple cloche hat for his model, pinning it up daily himself, like a milliner with feathers or plumes, creating new shapes and profiles.

Chihuly's work locates the magic and alchemy inherent in molten glass in gorgeous and permanent materiality. His work stands for change in constancy, highlights on surfaces of permanent fluidity, and cannot help but serve as an ethical standard for anyone who lives with it.

Henry Geldzahler

良質の新しいアートを見る喜びの一つは、規範を変えてしまう悪戯心に満ちたその能力にある。デイル・チフーリは心地良いカテゴリーの中に身を置くという罠に捕われることなく、複雑になりすぎたアートの世界に癒しをあたえている。

　まず、クラフトとアートとの境界を彼は自信に満ちて踏み越える。そして彼は、いまだかって抽象と具象との選択の必要を感じたことがない——すなわち自然と人工物との選択の必要に迫られたことはなかったのである。

　アートやクラフトという称号に内在する相対的ハイアラーキーについての混乱がアメリカには存在する。アーティストとかクラフトマンとかいうのはエゴを満たすためのカテゴリーであり、美学的差異にとって有用な、あるいは有意味なものではない。チフーリはたぐいまれな立場を占めている。彼の作品は時にはクラフトと共に、そして時にはアートギャラリーで画家や彫刻家の作品と共に展示される。木や、クレイや、ガラスで作られたその作品がこれら、クラフトとか、アートとかいった差別を無意味にしてしまう半ダースばかりの同時代の作家達の一翼をチフーリは担っている。もちろん、チフーリの作品をアメリカ、いや国際的なアートのコンテクストの下にとらえていくこの試みは、作品が呼び起こす素晴らしいヴィジュアルな衝撃に覚える関心からにほかならないのであるが。

　チフーリの作品を描こうとするとき、まず心に浮かぶイメージがある。それは微かに湾曲したハイライトを持つ流体運動の一様相を思い起こさせる。ニューヨーク、メトロポリタン美術館二十世紀部門の学芸員としてチフーリの作品と初めて出会ったときから、それは即座に記憶に残るものであり、また見る度ごとに一層の洗練を感じさせて

くれるものであった。それは力強く、美しく、素晴らしいことに常に進化し続けている。

　ガラス吹きのプロセスにチフーリはいつも取り憑かれているが、その作品はこのユニークな成型法の記録であるのみではない。それらは色彩と形とアーティストとの対話である。「ナバホ・シリンダー」から「ヴェネチアン」に至る進化の中で見せた鮮明で、新鮮な色彩の組み合わせの自由な探求、ガラスの透明な明るさとの戯れ、それらはガラスというこの未だ探求されていない素材を通して、彼にアートの歴史を付け加えさせた。

　チフーリが使用するもう一つの装飾法は「アド・オン」である。ガラスのコラージュ片が成型されたガラスに溶かし付けられる。ウィットに富んでいて、魅力的で、時にはドラマチックに、あるいはコミカルに、「アド・オン」は作品に合わせて使用される。それはマティスがニースの彼のホテルの部屋で、２０年代から３０年代にかけてずっとシンプルなクロシェ帽子を彼のモデルにかぶらせ、帽子屋が羽毛や羽飾りでするように自分で毎日ピンアップして、新しい形や姿を作っていたのを私に思いださせる。

　チフーリの作品は華美で永遠の物質性の下に、溶けたガラスに生来する魔術と練金術を見いだす。作品は恒久なるものの変化を示唆する、永遠の流動性の表面にハイライトを当てる。そして、それは視るもの全てに、一つの美的規範を与えざるを得ないものである。

ヘンリー・ゲルドザーラー

(元ニューヨーク近代美術館２０世紀部門学芸員)

NOW A SUPERSTAR in the world of glass, Dale Chihuly's first encounter with glass was in 1964. As an interior design student at the University of Washington, he wove glass into a tapestry, an unheard of juxtaposition of materials. After graduating, his fascination with glass continued and he discovered the precise and unforgiving process of glass blowing in a fateful event. One night in his basement studio, he melted some stained glass in a primitive kiln and with a pipe, blew a bubble. Miraculously it worked. Although people have blown glass for 2,000 years, often taking the process for granted, Chihuly marvels at the way air and molten glass collaborate to create a form. When heated glass becomes plastic and can be swollen by breath, deformed by gravity, and hardened by the simple lessening of heat.

Obsessed by this process, Chihuly went on to study with the "father" of the American Studio Glass Movement, Harvey Littleton at the University of Wisconsin, and continued at the Rhode Island School of Design. Baptized in the American Studio Glass Movement, he then won a Fulbright Fellowship, blessing him with a chance to see another world of glass. In 1968 he traveled to Venice to work on Murano with its jealously guarded secrets. He saw the ancient way of working with glass with teams of workers and he brought this knowledge back to the United States. He has enriched this tradition since all of *his* team members are artists as well as skilled artisans. Now no longer the master of the team, Chihuly's role is that of a choreographer who maps out the moves for his dancers.

A singular artist Chihuly has drawn from circumstance, the environment, and encounters with people and materials to create an outstanding body of work. Born on the Pacific rim in Washington state, he spent much time as a child with his family at the sea shore. He saw the great Puget Sound every day on his way to school. His mother would race with him and his older brother up hills to catch the technicolor sunsets of the Northwest. She also tended a flower garden full of riotous color. Knowing this helps us to understand some of the sources of Chihuly's imagination.

Before Chihuly embarked on the vessels that he is now world famous for, he experimented with the material of glass, exploiting its essential qualities. As a young teacher at the Rhode Island School of Design, he contrasted ice with neon, made room-sized sculptures of milk glass, and manipulated architectural space with glass panels. In the mid-1970's he began his explorations of the forms made naturally on the blow pipe. Listening to the very voice of the material, the shapes are spontaneous creations. "Follow nature" is the Chihuly team motto; in this way the distinctive Chihuly forms are born.

Chihuly's first series of vessels was the "Navajo Blanket Cylinders." In these he translated the woven textures of Indian weavings into glass by "picking up" "drawings" of glass shards and threads on the hot bubble of glass. He used the rounded forms as painter would canvas. The next series, the "Pilchuck Baskets," was also inspired by Native American imagery. He had seen some Northwest

いまやグラスアートのスーパースターとして世界に名を馳せるチフーリがはじめてガラスという素材と向き合ったのは、１９６４年、ワシントン大学のインテリア・デザインのコースでタペストリーのなかにガラス片を織り込もうと試みたときである。それはおよそ唐突とも思われる素材の選択であったが、その後、学校を卒業してからもガラスの魅力はひきつづき彼をとらえていった。ある夜、地下室のスタジオで、彼は吹きガラスの技法そのものを自分自身で発見するという衝撃的な体験をすることになる。チフーリは原始的なキルン（窯）でガラスを溶かし、パイプで息を吹き込んでみた。すると不思議にもパイプの先にうまく球ができたのである。チフーリは熱い可塑性のあるガラスが息を吹き込むことによって膨らみ、変形することに最大の関心を寄せるようになる。

チフーリは本格的にガラスを学ぶため、ウィスコンシン大学でスタジオ・グラス運動の父ともいえるハーヴィ・リトルトンに師事し、さらにロード・アイランド・デザイン美術学校で修学を続ける。こうしてチフーリはスタジオ・グラス運動の洗礼を受け、一方で、もう一つのガラスの世界を見る機会に恵まれる。１９６８年、フルブライトの奨学金を得て、ガラス制作の伝統を誇るヴェネツィア、ムラノ島に留学し、アメリカ人としてははじめてヴェニーニ工房で研鑽を積むことになる。連綿と伝統を受け継いできたヴェネツィアの職人達の見事なチームプレイを目のあたりにし、その知識をアメリカへと持ち帰ることになる。

氷とネオンを組み合せた作品、室内空間を満たす乳白グラスのオブジェ、建築空間に設置するグラス・パネル…。いくつかの実験的試みののち、１９７０年代半ばころより、ブロー・パイプ（宙吹きのための吹き竿）から自然に導かれる形の探求を始めていく。空気の力で膨らみ、重力の作用を受けて変形し、遠心力によって広がる。そして温度の低下にしたがってその動きが凍結する。そうした素材の自然の声を聞きながら、"Follow Nature" つまり、自然であることをモットーにいくつもの豊かなヴァリエーションを生みだしてゆくのである。

最初の器のシリーズ「ナバホ・ブランケット（Navajo Blanket Cylinders）」はナバホ・インディアンのブランケットに着想を得たもので、熱いガラスの表面にガラス片やガラス棒を組み合せて熔着し、織物のテクスチュアを表現しようとしている。まるい器の形はチフーリにとってのキャンバスとなっている。次のシリーズ「ピルチャック・バスケット（Pilchuck Baskets）」もまたナバホ・インディアンのバスケットがヒントになっている。たまたまワシントン州立歴史協会で、ノースウェスト沿岸地方のインディアンたちのバスケットが無造作に積み重ねられ、それ自体の重さでたれさがり、時間の経過でゆがんでいるのを新鮮な驚きをもって見たのである。

このアース・トーンの有機的なバスケットの形はやがて「シー・フォーム（Sea Forms）」シリーズへと展開していく。それはけっして自然界の姿が具体的に描写されているわけではないが、自然の形としかいいようのないものである。そして、続く「マキア（Macchia）」シリーズでは、既に獲得した自然なフォルムのうえに、できうる限りの色彩の美しさを引き出す試みが繰り返されている。外側の斑文と内側の色彩がコントラストをなし、さらにアクセントとなる鮮やかな色の縁取りが全体をひきしめている。このような多彩な色の組み合せは技術的にはきわめて困難であるにもかかわらず、それが克服されているのである。いつもながらの「チフーリ・マジック」である。

ひとりの芸術家にとって、その境遇や人格を育んだ環境、人やものとの出会いが、その創作活動

Coast Indian baskets casually stacked inside each other in storage at the Washington State Historical Society, sagging under their own weight, distorted by age and gravity. The organic forms of the "Baskets" with their earth tones then evolved into the "Sea Forms." Though not exact representations of nature, they were nothing if not natural. These were followed by the "Macchia," endlessly amazing combinations of raucous color presented in the shapes perfected in the previous series: Interiors contrast with their mottled exteriors; lip wraps of yet another hue add a linear accent to the full forms. Technically this layering of color should not work, but with the typical Chihuly magic, the pieces survive their making.

In the next development, the "Persians," the color was more controlled and for the first time in his career, Chihuly created a more ordered patterning. Colors still confront each other in ways that take one's breath away: cobalt blues with maize yellows, acid greens against terra cotta reds, and saffron with lapis; but instead of exuberant expressionistic compositions, the patterns are strict, yet exotic stripes and spirals of color. Like ancient treasure the "Persians" seem to be flotsam washed to Nature's breast, floating from distant lands, sparkling at times in the dawn light, at others in the setting sun. Chihuly's most recent series, the "Venetians," was inspired by the glass of the Art Deco period in Venice. A radical change from the undulating forms of the earlier works, they are busy and decorative. They hark back to the *Carnevale* of misty Venetian withers with revellers in ethereal masks and costumes.

Chihuly's impact on the glass world goes beyond this amazing body of work. In fact, his oeuvre would have been impossible without the team, the concept he considers his most significant contribution to glass. Throughout his career, Chihuly has committed himself to sharing the knowledge of glass-working techniques. This is an American approach that contrasts with what he saw on Murano with its cloistered artisans to whom nothing was more terrible than the loss of their secrets.

Another of Chihuly's proud achievements is the Pilchuck Glass School, north of Seattle. It was co-founded by Chihuly with the Northwest art patrons Anne Gould Hauberg and John Hauberg in 1971. Teachers from around the world come every summer to sharpen the skills of students. However, the school does not simply dispense technical knowledge; it fosters experimentation. Who can say how many young artists have been launched by the activities of Pilchuck.

Chihuly, like the material he has chosen to work with, is always in motion. Never content to stay in one place, he travels widely. Never satisfied with his aesthetic triumphs, he experiments constantly. Where the creative imagination is concerned, Chihuly does not know the meaning of the word stop.

Yoriko Mizuta
(Translated by Ian Perlman and Karen Chambers)

に直接、間接的に大きな影響を及ぼすことは異論のないところであろう。チフーリは太平洋岸のワシントン州タコマに生まれ、しばしば家族とともに海辺で遊んだ。学校の行き帰りには雄大な景色を見て育った。時には母や弟と共にノースウェストのまばゆいばかりの日没を追いかけて、丘まで駆けたりした。その母は色鮮やかな花を育てる花園をつくっていた。そうしたことからも、豊かに広がるチフーリのイメージのよって来るところがおのずと理解できるように思われるのである。

「パージャン（Persians）」シリーズではさらに洗練された色の組み合せで、ドラマチックに色を対峙させて見るものに息を飲ませる。コバルト・ブルーとイェロー、グリーンとテラコッタの赤…。エキゾチックで華やかであるが、縞や渦巻きのパターンは緻密で厳格である。それらは古代の宝物のようでもあり、あるいは、自然の懐に打ち寄せられた貝殻や遠く異国から流れついた漂流物が、時には朝日、時には夕陽を受けてきらきらと輝いているように見える。

最新のシリーズである「ヴェニーシアン（Venetians）」は、ヴェネツィアのアール・デコ時代のガラスに触発されており、それまでのシリーズから一転してラジカルな変化を遂げている。そのにぎやかで装飾的な様式は、ヴェネツィアの冬のカーニバルの耽美的な仮面や仮装用の衣装をほうふつとさせるところがある。

チフーリはこれらの驚くべき作品群の制作を独自のチームを結成して推し進めてきた。すべての作品はこのチームを抜きに考えることはできない。チームのメンバーはみな、熟練の技を持ち、同時におのおのが独立した作家でもある。チフーリの作品を作るときは、それぞれの持ち場でそれぞれの役割を果たし、チフーリはメンバーを動かす振り付け師となって作品に息を吹き込むのであ

る。こうしたチームのコンセプトこそ、チフーリが新しいガラス芸術に大きな可能性をもたらしたもっとも重要な点である。長年にわたる制作を通じて、チフーリはガラス制作の知識をすすんで皆に分け与えてきた。これはかつてムラノで見た、かたくなにガラス制作の秘密を守る閉鎖的な職人の世界からすれば、きわめてアメリカ的なアプローチといえよう。

チフーリを語るうえで、ピルチャック・スクールのことにも触れないわけにはいかない。これはノースウェストの芸術篤志家、アン・ハウバーグとジョン・ハウバーグの助けを得て、チフーリが１９７１年に作った学校である。毎年夏には各国の優れた講師陣を迎え、アメリカ国内ばかりでなく、世界中のガラスを志す若い人々に研修の機会を提供している。ここではさまざまなテクニックが公開されるばかりでなく、数多くの実験的試みが繰り広げられている。このピルチャック・スクールがどれほど多くの若い作家達を育て、勇気を与えてきたかわからない。

チフーリはいつもひとつのところに留まってはいない。大きな成功を勝ちとっても決してそれに満足することなく、常に実験を続けている。創造的なイマジネーションの世界で、チフーリはまだまだ行き着くところを知らないようである。

水田順子
(北海道立近代美術館主任学芸員)

バスケット

1977年の夏、私はイタロ・スカンガと共にタコマ歴史資料館を訪れ、そこでノースウェスト・コースト・インディアンたちの手によるバスケットが幾重にも重ねられて展示されているのを見て、強い衝撃を受けたことを憶えている。それらは凹まされていたり、湾曲させられた、素晴らしいフォルムだった。なぜそれをガラスで作ってみようと思ったのか自分でもよく分からないが、しかし、それがその夏の私の使命となった。

デイル・チフリー

バスケット・シリーズ全般において、チフリーは淡い色使いに甘んじ細い線によって形を浮き出させることを控えている。多くの場合、線状の要素は対照的ではあるが本体と深いつながりのある色によって縁をいろどり、不揃いな楕円の口を強調するためだけにとどめられている。他の物ではデリケートな何本もの平行線が作品を取りまいている。そこには常にフォルムとそれを強調する糸状の線との完全な調和が有る。

マイケル・モンロー
(スミソニアン・インスティチュート学芸員)

BASKETS

In the summer of 1977, I was visiting the Tacoma Historical Society with Italo Scanga, and I remember being struck by a pile of Northwest Coast Indian baskets that were stacked one inside another. They were dented and misshapen, wonderful forms. I don't really know what made me want to reproduce them in glass, but that was my mission for the summer.

Dale Chihuly

Throughout the Basket Series, Chihuly consistently resorts to subtle use of color and restraint in his description of the shapes through the use of line. Often the linear element is limited to a lip wrap of a contrasting but closely related color to emphasize the uneven ellipse of the glass baskets. In other pieces, a delicate tracery of several parallel lines circumscribes the form. Always there is a total fusion of the threadlike lines with the forms they describe.

Michael Monroe

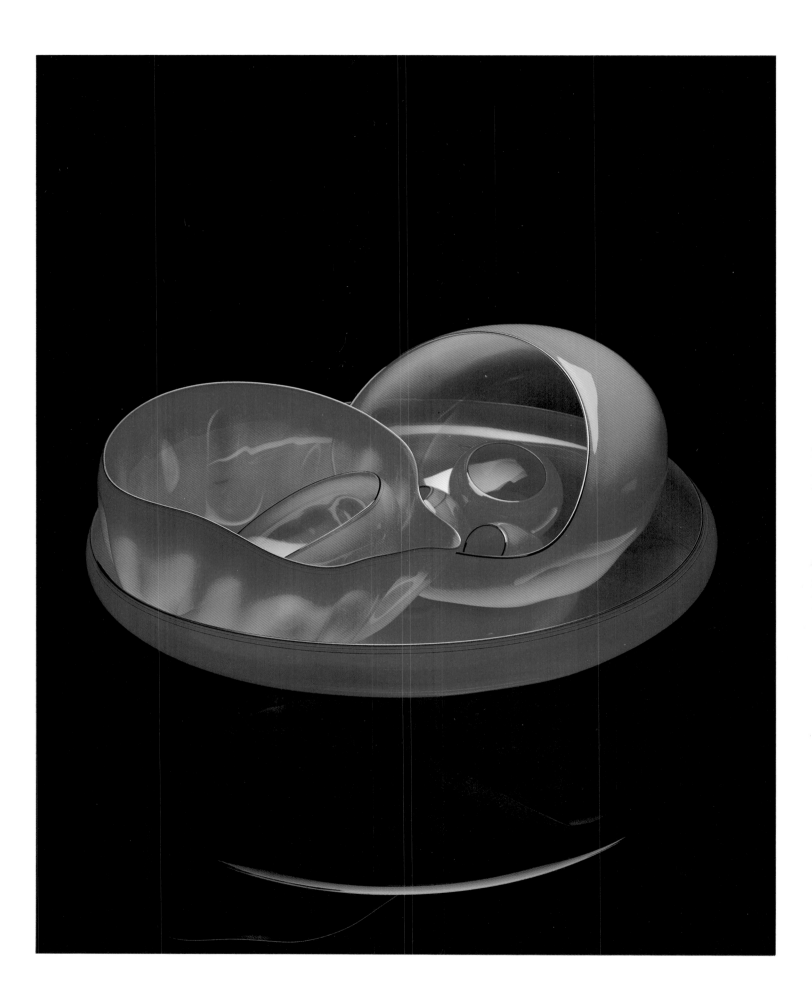

シー・フォーム

1977年の「ピルチャック・バスケット」シリーズに始まるチフリーの完成度の高い仕事は、彼が1981年に制作した「シー・フォーム」によって彫刻的要素、透明感、形など、全てにおいて頂点に達した。この作品はフォルムや制作において、その限界まで追求し、多作なこの作家の最も名人芸的なところを見せている。溶けたガラスは繊細な色使いの細かい線でレースのように包み込まれ、驚くほど薄い貝殻に作り上げられていく。それが冷めた後、さながら珍しい貝か、熱帯の海洋植物か、揺らめくクラゲのごとく、ドラマチックなグループに組み合わされる。

ジャック・コワート

(ワシントン国立美術ギャラリー２０世紀部門学芸員)

SEA FORMS

Chihuly's mature work, beginning with the "Pilchuck Basket" series in 1977, reaches a pinnacle of sculptural reflection, transparency, and shape in his 1981, "Sea Forms". These works push at the limits of form and production, and show the prolific artist at this most virtuoso. The molten glass is laced with delicately colored threads, . . . spun into frighteningly thin shells . . . and, after cooling, nested together in dramatic groups like rare shells, tropical sea vegetation, or floating jellyfish.

Jack Cowart

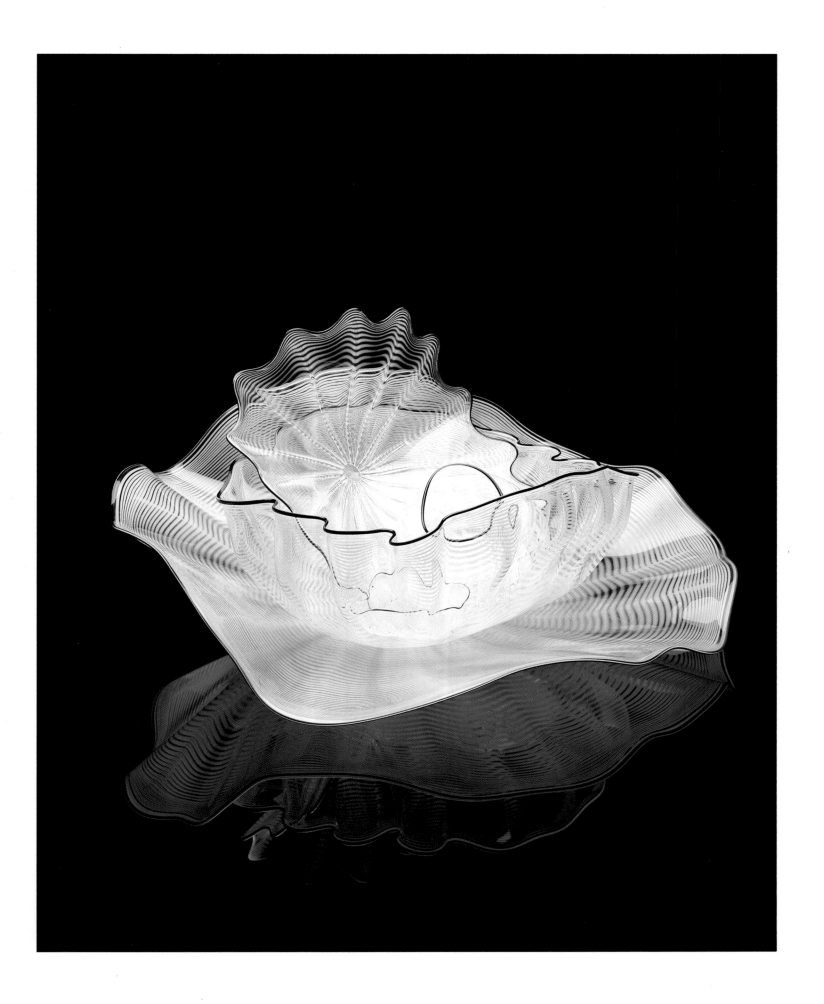

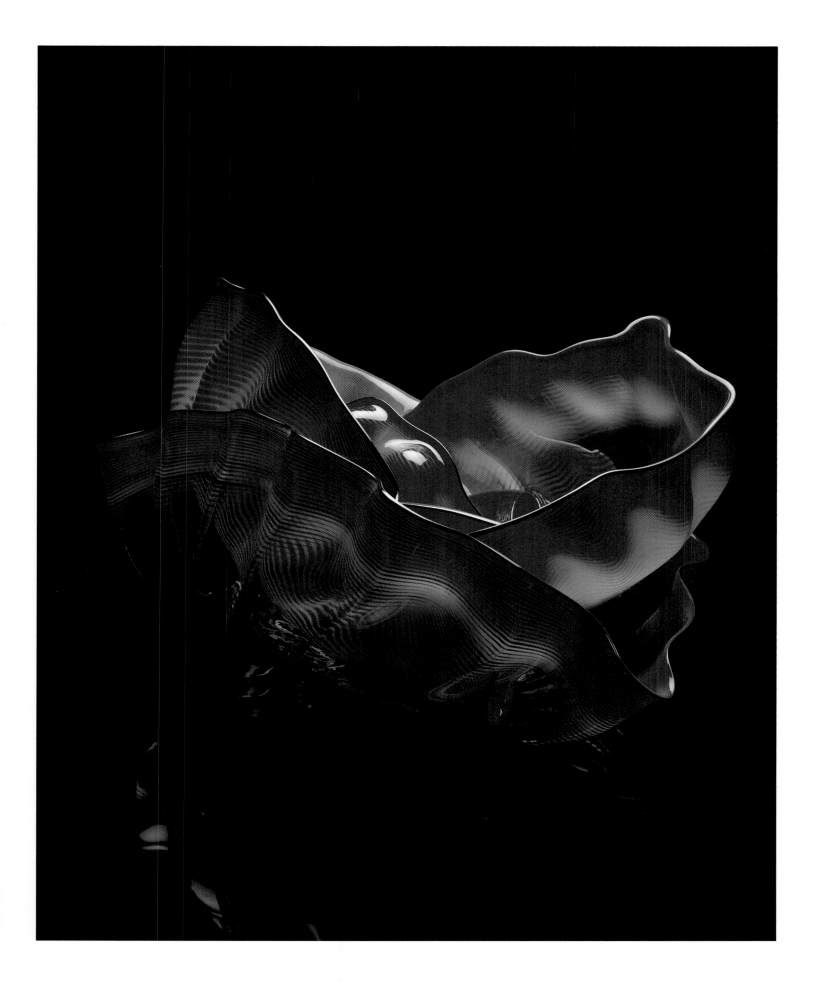

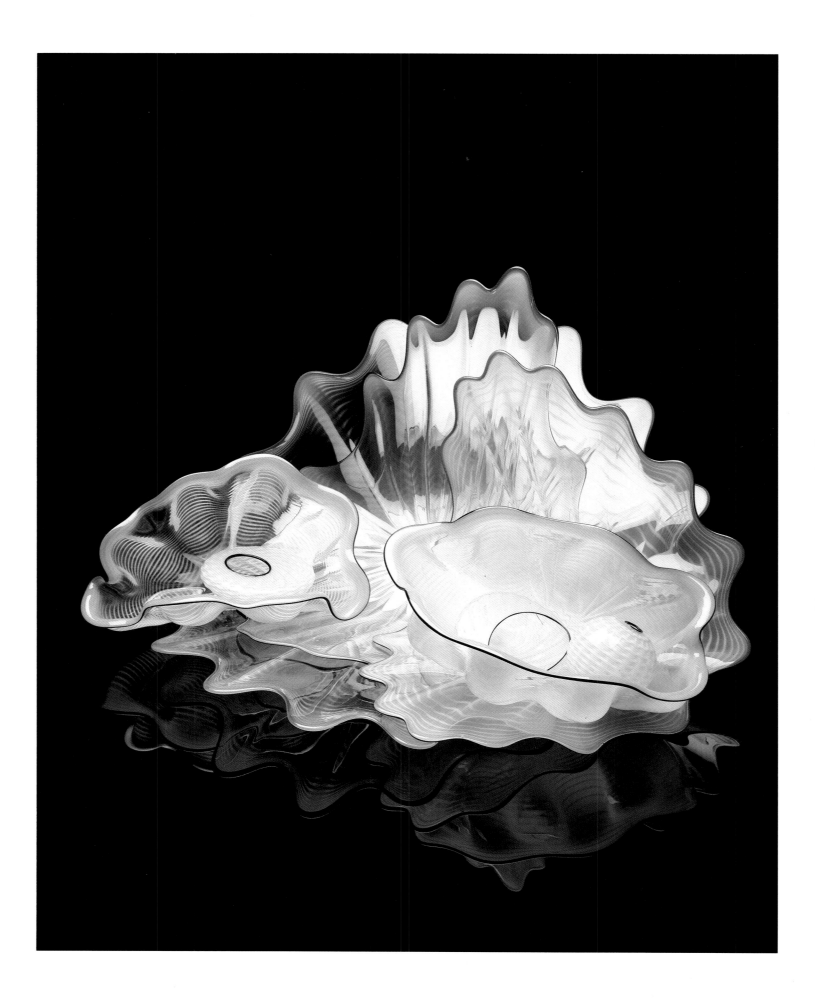

ソフトシリンダー

「ピルチャック・シリンダー」シリーズのガラスを吹く過程で施された模様は、新しく、今まで以上に複雑で精密であり、以前に比べてはるかに衝動的で力強いイメージを表現している。それはただの表面処理に終わっていない。大きな線状のモチーフは、ガラスの中に入り込み、動きのある内面を作り出し、この作品の表現力に富んだ雰囲気をよりいっそう引き立てている。

マイケル・モンロー
(スミソニアン・インスティチュート学芸員)

SOFT CYLINDERS

The "glass drawings" on the "Pilchuck Cylinders" divulge new and greater degrees of complexity and control, aggressive images that are considerably more spontaneous than before. . . .There is no surface decoration here. The larger linear imagery has penetrated the glass creating an animated interior layer that complements and intensifies the expressive mood of these pieces.

Michael Monroe

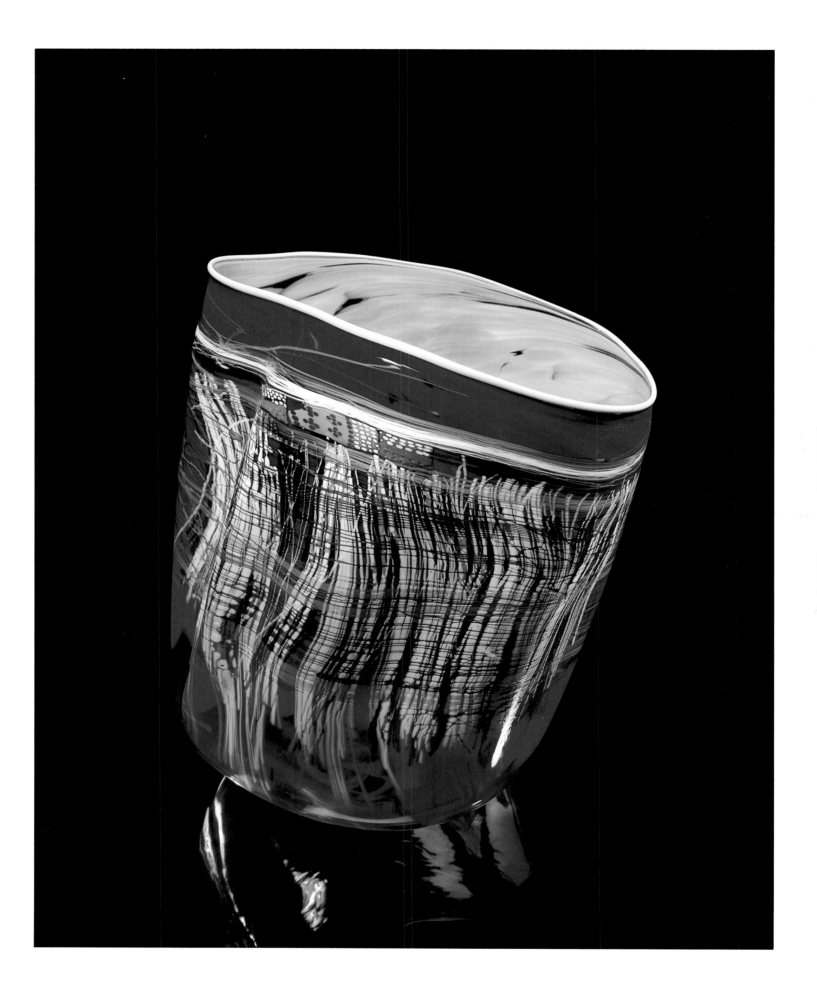

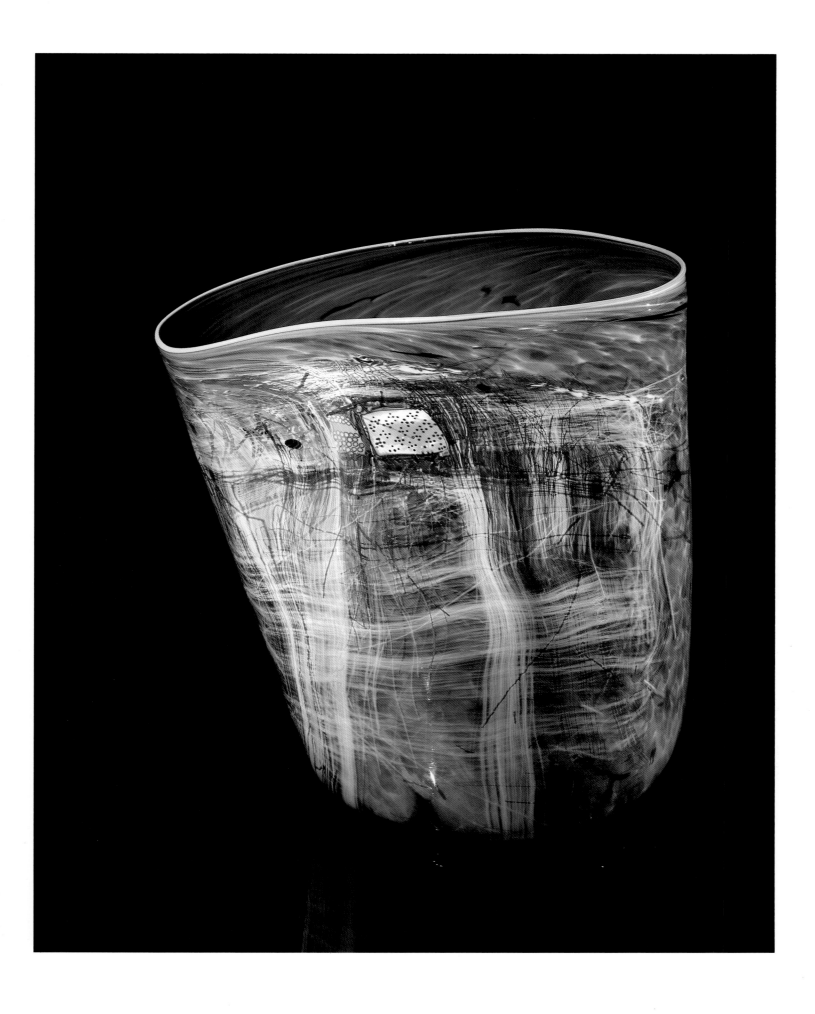

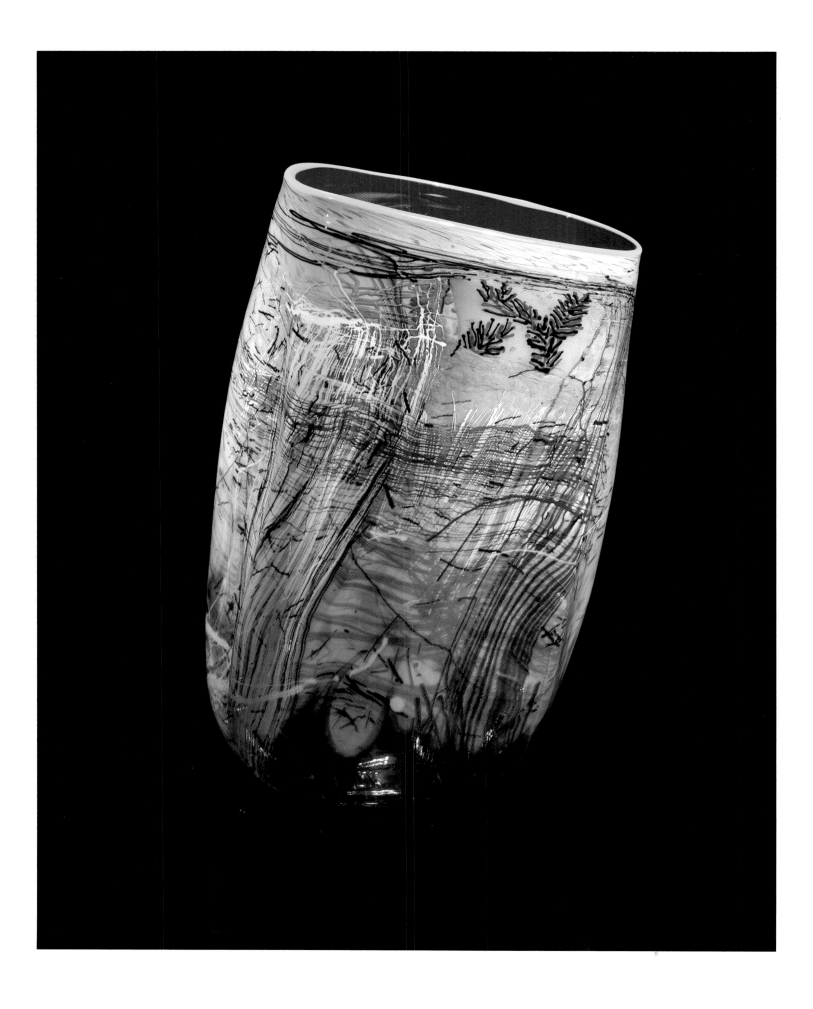

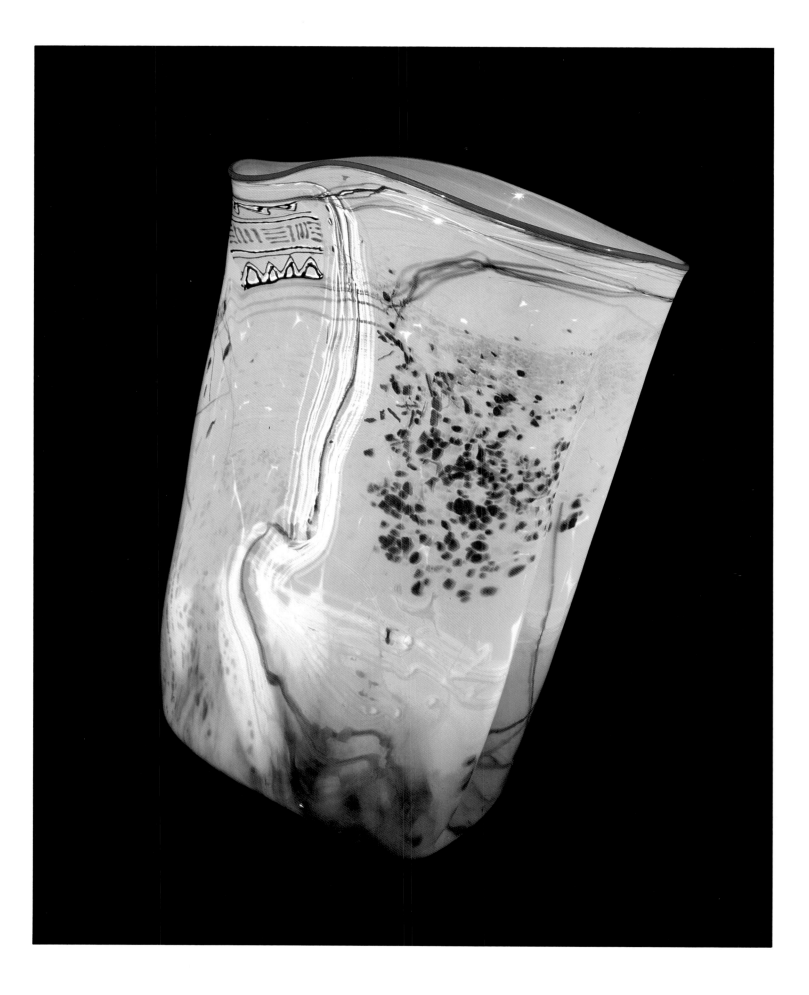

マキア

チフリーの「マキア」シリーズほどの大きさになると、ガラスのオブジェは新たな存在になる。ガラスはその純潔さやナイーヴさを失ってしまったように見える。それは壊れやすいものであることに変わりはないが、もはや慎ましやかで押しつけがましくなく、儚いものであることを装う必要はない。このシリーズでチフリーは、作品がまだ柔らかく、固まりきっていない出来上がりつつある瞬間を捕えようとしている。この大きな作品の波のような縁、鮮やかな曲線のアウトライン、縞模様、激しいまだら模様の色などは、全て生命を宿し、息をし、脈うつ巨大なフォルムを思わせる。内部空間が躍動を生み出し、作品に一つの形を与えている。それは奇妙であるが、拒否しがたいものである。絶大な力を持つ予期せぬ砂漠の竜巻のように「マキア」は次のメタモルフォーゼにより、別の形になるための準備をして、束の間の危ういバランスを保っているように見える。この作品によって私たちはガラスが凍った液体であり、物質の一時的な状態であることを再確認させられる。

ロバート・ホッブス

(美術史家)

MACCHIA

When glass objects reach the scale of Chihuly's "Macchia" series, a new identity is achieved. Glass appears to have lost its innocence and naivete; it no longer has to pretend to be unassuming, undemanding and fragile, even though it continues to play on ephemerality. . . .In this series, Chihuly attempts to catch the formulative moment, the time when creation is happening; when it is still fluid and not yet congealed. Ruffled edges, whiplash outlines, striation, and intense, mottled colors in these large pieces all call to mind living, breathing, pulsating forms of monumental proportions. . . .An inner space activates them, giving shape to the entire series; it is whimsical and yet inexorable. Like a dust devil on the desert, an unpredictable whirlwind capable of great force, the "Macchia" appear to have reached only a momentary, tentative balance, ready to move on to assume another shape, another metamorphosis. They remind us that glass is a frozen liquid, a transient state of matter.

Robert Hobbs

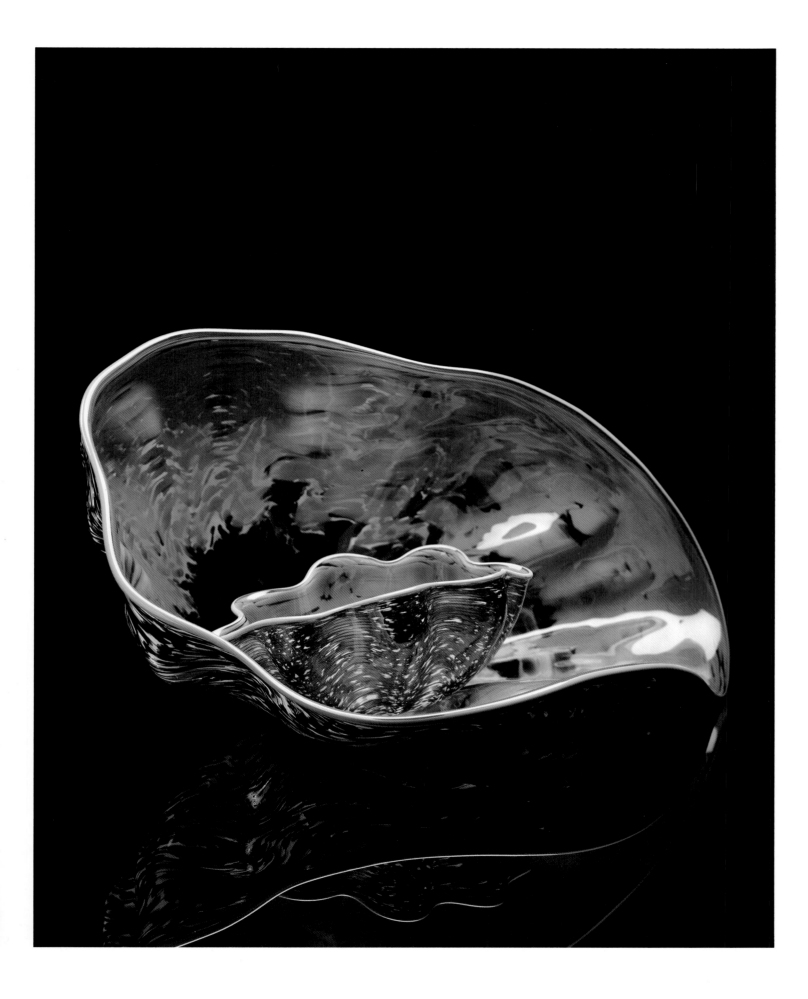

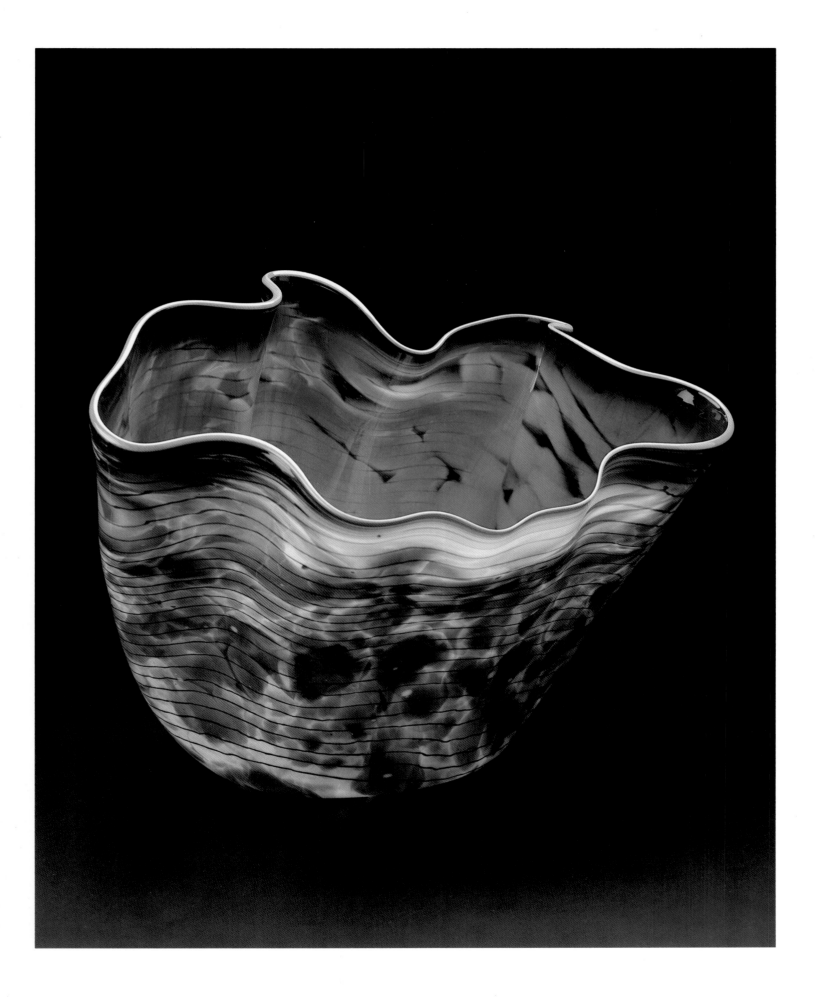

ペルシャン

エレガントだが不思議な違和感のある「ペルシャン」シリーズでは、デイル・チフリーは、奇跡を求めている。「ペルシャン」を構成するそれぞれのパーツは深く考え抜かれて作られている。各パーツは、「バスケット」シリーズや「シーフォーム」シリーズで折り紙付きの評価を得た特色ある織目模様と、ヴェネチアングラスの糸状の繊細な美しさを合わせ持っている。

しかし、これらの初期のシリーズと違って「ペルシャン」には、掘り出された宝物のような雰囲気がある。器の口はさまざまな形に広げられ、古代の香水ビンを思わせるボトルネックは驚くほどの柔軟性をもって引き延ばされている。大きなタザ（tazzas）は、それを取りつけるガラスのステムがまだ熱くポンテに付いている時点で形づくられるため、引力の力に優雅に服従し、必然的に傾き、ねじれ、曲がる。

ロバート・ホップス
(美術史家)

PERSIANS

In his elegant yet strangely disturbing series of "Persians," Dale Chihuly courts the miraculous.   Each element making up the "Persians" is intensely conceived: The pieces combine the delicacy of threaded Venetian glass with the distinctive woven patterns that are the hallmark of his "Baskets" and "Sea Forms".   But unlike these earlier series the "Persians" suggest found treasure.   . . .Their variously shaped orifices are dilated; the necks of bottles, which resemble ancient perfume containers, stretch forth with wondrous elasticity; and huge tazzas, still attached to the glass stems which held them to pontil rods while they were being formed, have gracefully succumbed to gravity, and consequently lean, twist, and turn.

Robert Hobbs

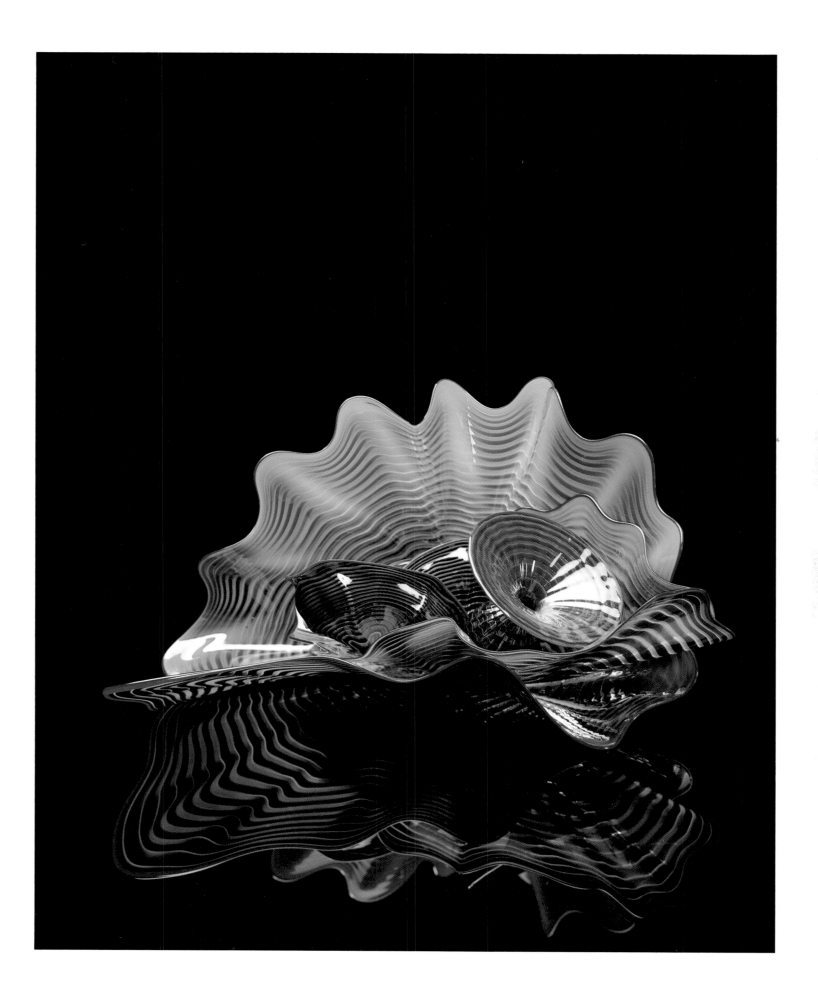

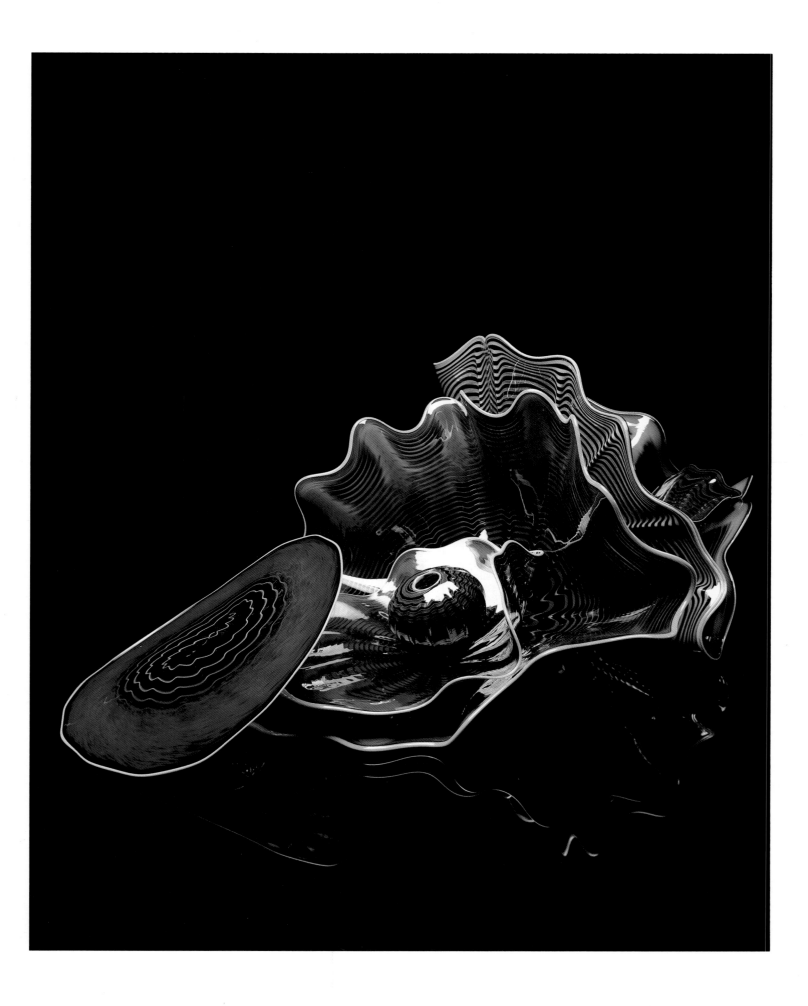

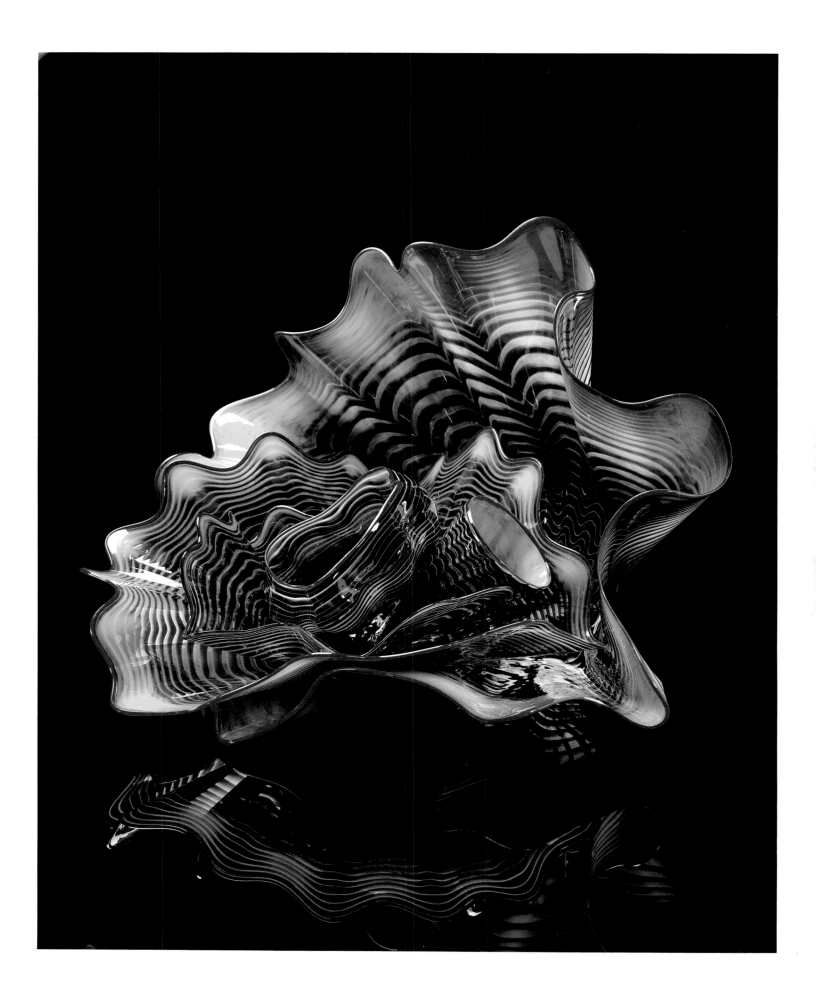

ヴェネチアン

「ヴェネチアン」にはいつも緊張感が付きまとう。クラシックなフォルムは有機的な力によって容赦なくその実直さを侵害される。全ての装飾がそういう流れを暗示している。

熱いガラスは、自然の法則と流動する現実に翻弄され自らを装う。引力の物理的な力は個性的なバイタリズムを示唆するために味方につけられ、あるいは挑まれて利用される。その流動性と作業の自然さは生物の神秘的なメタモルフォーゼに等しい。植物的で生物的形態を持つ装飾は自然の摂理を肯定しているようでもあり、否定しているようでもある。作品はまるで生きて成長しているかのようにまわりの空間を侵略し、自らを拡張する。「ヴェネチアン」を構成する生き物のようなそれぞれの作品は、チフリーの他のシリーズよりはるかに人格と言ってもよいような強い個性を持っている。

ロン・グロウェン
(コーニッシュ美術大学美術史講師、美術評論家)

VENETIANS

Tensions abound in the "Venetians". Every attachment seems to indicate flux, a relentless organic force impinging on the physical integrity of the classic form. Hot glass simulates or is affected by natural properties and realities — its fluidity and the spontaneity of working equates to the mysterious metamorphoses of living organisms, while physical forces of gravity can be utilized or challenged to suggest an independent vitalism. The vegetative and biomorphic decoration and ornamentation of the "Venetians" seem to both confirm and contradict the laws of nature. The works expand aggressively into space, like a living and growing thing. And like living things, each work of the "Venetians" has an individual character, a personality if you will, much more so than Chihuly's other series.

Ron Glowen

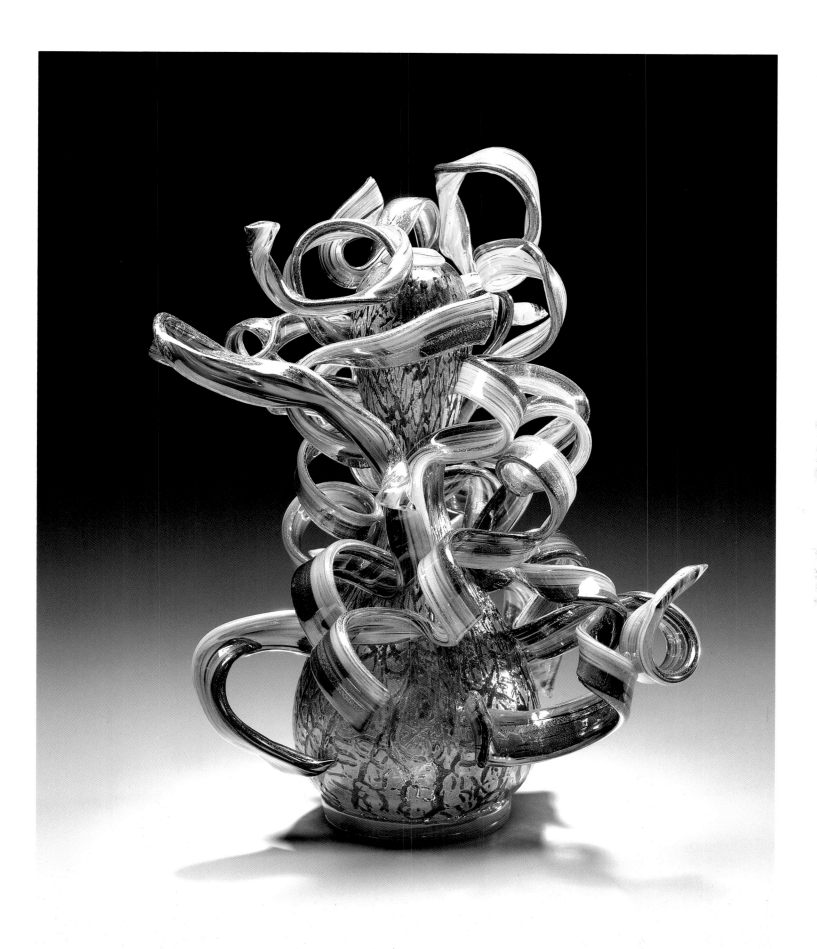

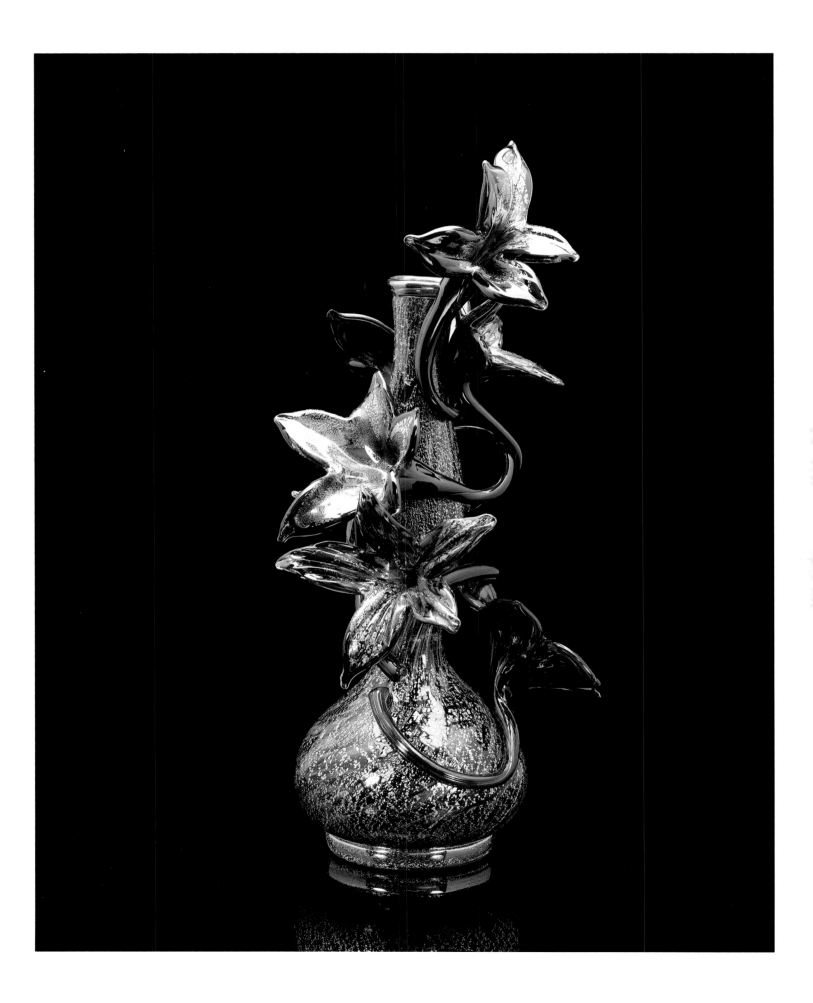

ドローイング

すばやく器の輪郭の線を描き、豆や小石や貝殻など、凹凸のある表面をもっている物で利用できるものは何でも敷きつめ、その上をなぞって描く。こうしてチフリーはマキア・シリーズのまだら模様の色を表現する

カレン・S・チェンバース

(美術評論家、ニューワーク誌元編集長)

ヴェネチアンの仕事に入って4、5日過ぎた頃、彼は木炭による大胆なドローイングを描き始めた。それは、これまでのグラファイトや色エンピツによる彼特有の軽やかなドローイングに比べてより厳しくはっきりしたものであった。そうして生み出されたシリーズ「ヴェネチアン」は、より異国情緒豊かなものになった。

今までのチフリーの仕事に比べるとヴェネチアンは、驚くほど異質である。クラシックなフォルムこそ、伝統にのっとりシンメトリカルであるかもしれない。しかし大げさで騒々しい器には伝統的な要素はみじんも無く、突飛な装飾がほどこされ、誘惑的な色使いがなされている。

ディヴィッド・バードン

(美術評論家)

DRAWINGS

Swooping lines outline the vessels, and by drawing over a bed of dried beans, small pebbles, or sea shells — anything available to provide an agitated surface, Chihuly approximates the splotches of color of the "Macchia" series.

Karen S. Chambers

By the fourth or fifth day of working the "Venetians", he started to make bold drawings in charcoal, much harsher and more explicit than his typically ethereal drawings in graphite and colored pencil; and the resulting series of works — the "Venetians", became progressively more outlandish.

The "Venetians" differ startlingly from most of Chihuly's previous work. The classical forms may be more traditionally symmetrical, but there is nothing conventional about these grandiose and boisterous vessels with their outrageous ornamentation and their rousing colors. . .

David Bourdon

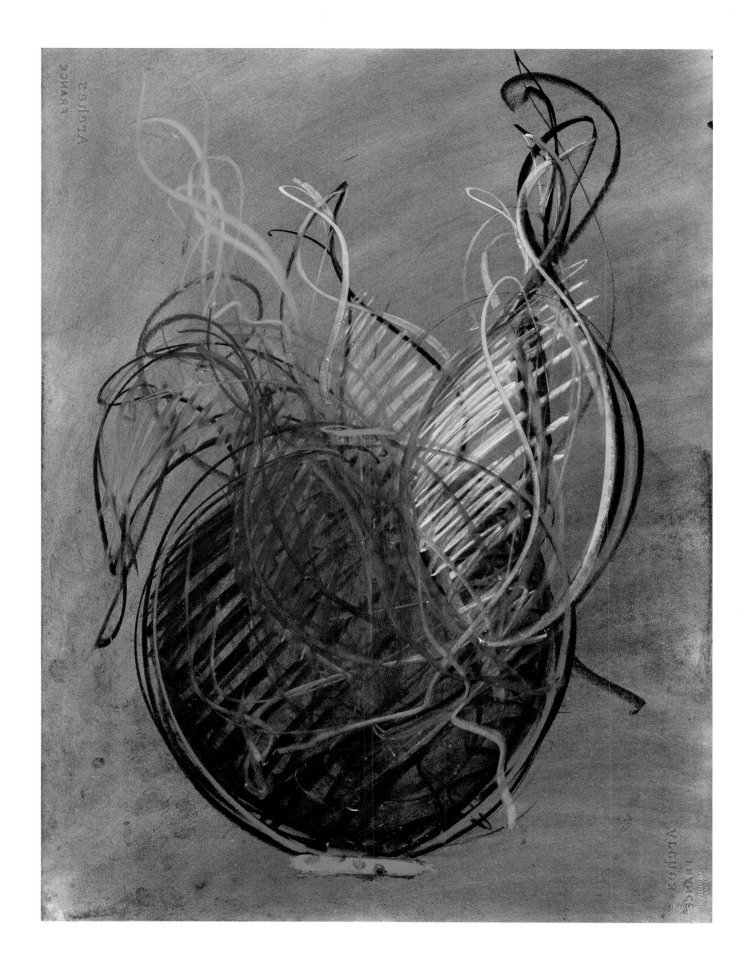

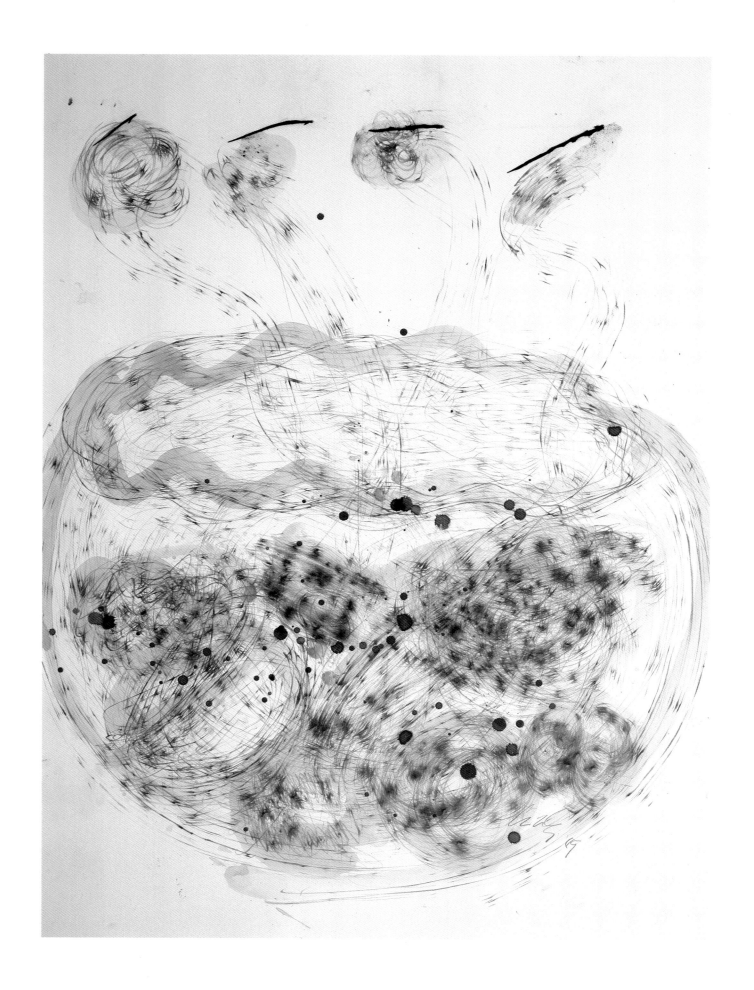

インスタレーション

3年ほど前、ヘンリー・ゲルドザーラーを通じてコミッションを得ることがあった。ロックフェラーセンターのレインボールームに取付ける大きなプロジェクトだった。そのときから、プライベートのものやら公共空間に入ったものを含め、15ものインスタレーションを完成してきた。自分自身が建築畑の出身のせいか、空間と光への関心は常に持っており、レインボウルームのプロジェクトの後、壁から浮かび上がってくるような大きな吹きガラスのフォルムを使っての仕事を続けた。ガラスを壁に取付ける新しい方法を自ら開発し、最近ではピースの背後に小さな低電圧スポットライトを取付け、ガラスを通じた光線を映しだすという手法を考案した。バックライティングのほかに天井からも光を当て、フルカラーの影を映しだす。それは壁を満たし、コンポジションを引き伸ばす。

これらのプロジェクトはいままで試みた中でも最もチャレンジングなものであった。直径5フィートにもなる吹きガラスのフォルムに理想のライティングを与える。それはもう夢が現実になることだと言ってもいい。何時か完璧な場所に、一層大きい吹きガラスのフォルムで、ビルディング中の全てをデザインする日を夢想する。

デイル・チフリー

INSTALLATIONS

Three years ago I was commissioned through Henry Geldzahler to do a large project for the Rainbow Room Complex at Rockefeller Center. I have completed about 15 installations since then in both private and public spaces. With my background in architecture I have always been interested in space and light so after the Rainbow Room project I continued to work with large blown glass forms that float off the wall. We developed new ways to attach the glass to the wall and more recently invented a technique to add small low voltage spotlights that are placed behind pieces to project light through the glass. In addition to the back-lighting we project light from the ceiling to create full color shadows that flood the wall and stretch the composition.

These projects are the most challenging work I have done to date, pushing the blown forms up to five feet in diameter with the ideal solution in lighting. You might say, it's a dream come true. I fantasize that some day I might design an entire building utilizing even larger blown forms in the perfect space.

Dale Chihuly

Budget —
25,000 a piece

1 Pair 40-45,000

BIOGRAPHY

Born in Tacoma, Washington, September 21, 1941

EDUCATION

1968
M.F.A., Rhode Island School of Design,
Providence, Rhode Island

1967
M.S., University of Wisconsin, Madison, Wisconsin

1965
B.A., University of Washington, Seattle, Washington

AWARDS

1988
Honorary Doctorate, California College of Arts and
Crafts, Oakland, California

1987
Governor's Writers Award, Washington
University of Washington Alumni Legend, Seattle,
Washington

1986
Honorary Doctorate, University of Puget Sound, Tacoma,
Washington
Honorary Doctorate, Rhode Island School of Design,
Providence, Rhode Island

1985
Governor's Art Award, Washington

1984
Rhode Island School of Design, President's Fellow,
Providence, Rhode Island
American Council for the Arts, Visual Artist's Award,
New York
Governor's Art Award, Washington (with Pilchuck Glass
School)

1977
National Endowment for the Arts Fellowship

1975
National Endowment for the Arts Fellowship

1968
Fulbright Fellowship to Murano, Italy

1967
Louis Comfort Tiffany Foundation Award

1964
Seattle Weavers Guild

SELECTED ONE-MAN MUSEUM EXHIBITIONS

1990
The Azabu Museum of Arts and Crafts

1989
Museum Boymans-van Beuningen, Rotterdam,
The Netherlands
Israel Museum, Jerusalem
The Society for Art in Crafts, Pittsburgh, Pennsylvania
Kalamazoo Institute of Arts, Kalamazoo, Michigan
Sao Paulo Bienal, Museum of Modern Art, Sao Paulo, Brazil

1988
Fabrica Escola Stephens, Marinha Grande, Portugal
Gulbenkian Foundation, Lisbon, Portugal
Musee Unterlinden, Colmar, France
Dia Art Foundation, Bridgehampton, New York

1987
Musee Matisse, Chateau-Cambresis, France
Museum of Art, University of Oklahoma, Norman,
Oklahoma
Roanoke Museum, Roanoke, Virginia

1986
Brunnier Gallery and Museum, Ames, Iowa
Chicago Public Library Cultural Center, Chicago, Illinois
The Mint Museum of Art, Charlotte, North Carolina
Musee des Arts Decoratifs, Paris, France
Muskegon Museum of Art, Muskegan, Michigan
Museum of Decorative Arts, Montreal, Quebec, Canada

1985
The Arkansas Art Center, Little Rock, Arkansas
Illinois State University Art Museum, Normal, Illinois
Madison Art Center, Madison, Wisconsin
Pennsylvania State University Museum of Art,
University Park, Pennsylvania

1984
Bellevue Art Museum, Bell, Washington
Crocker Art Museum, Sacramento, California
Forth Worth Art Museum, Texas

1983
The St. Louis Art Museum, St. Louis, Missouri
Palm Spring Desert Museum, Palm Springs, California
Providence Art Club, Providence, Rhode Island

1982
Phoenix Art Museum, Phoenix, Arizona
Tucson Museum of Art, Tucson, Arizona
San Diego Museum of Art, San Diego, California

1981
Lobmeyr Museum, Vienna, Austria
Tacoma Art Museum, Tacoma, Washington

1980
Haaretz Museum, Tel Aviv, Israel
University of Rhode Island Art Gallery, Kingston,
Rhode Island

1979
Lobmeyr Museum, Vienna, Austria
Museu de Arte, Sao Paulo, Brazil

1978
Renwick Gallery, Smithsonian Institution, Washington, D.C.
Galerie der Kunsthandwerber, Hamburg, West Germany

1977
Yuma Fine Arts Association, Yuma, Arizona
University of Minnesota, St. Paul, Minnesota

1976
Bell Gallery, Brown University, Providence, Rhode Island
Wadsworth Atheneum, Hartford, Connecticut
Leigh Yawkey Woodson Art Museum, Wausau, Wisconsin

1975
Utah Museum of Fine Arts, Salt Lake City, Utah
Institute of American Indian Arts, Santa Fe, New Mexico

1971
American Craft Museum, New York City, New York

1967
University of Wisconsin, Madison, Wisconsin

COMMISSIONED ARCHITECTURAL INSTALLATIONS

1984 - 1989

Mr. and Mrs. Irvin Borowsky, Philadelphia, Pennsylvania
Chancellor Park, La Jolla, California
Mr. and Mrs. Norman Cohn, Philadelphia, Pennsylvania
Frank Russell Building, Tacoma, Washington
Hill Haven Corporation, Tacoma, Washington
Hyatt Hotel, Adelaide, Australia
IBM Corporation, New York City, New York
First Interstate World Center, Los Angeles, California
Fleet Bank, Providence, Rhode Island
Frances and Sydney Lewis Foundation, Richmond, Virginia
Madison Stouffer Hotel, Seattle, Washington
Oceanic Grace Yacht, Tokyo, Japan
Pacific First Center, Seattle, Washington
Rainbow Pavillion, Rockefeller Center, New York City,
New York
Seattle Aquarium, Seattle, Washington
Sheraton Hotel, Tacoma, Washington
Sheraton Hotel and Towers, Seattle, Washington
Mr. and Mrs. Jon Shirley, Bellevue, Washington
Swedish Hospital, Seattle, Washington
Tacoma Art Museum, Tacoma, Washington
Tacoma Financial Center, Tacoma, Washington
United States Customs, Blaine, Washington

SELECTED PUBLIC COLLECTIONS

Australian Arts Council, Sydney, Australia
Bass Brothers Enterprises, Fort Worth, Texas
California College of Arts and Crafts, Oakland, California
Chase Manhattan Bank, New York City, New York
Columbia Tower Club, Seattle, Washington
Foster and Marshall, Incorporated, Spokane, Washington
Harold Hess Company, Incorporated, Philadelphia,
Pennsylvania
The Hearn Company, Chicago, Illinois
IBM Corporation, New York City, New York
Johnson Wax Collection, Racine, Wisconsin
Niijima Glass School, Niijima, Japan
Pilchuck Glass School, Stanwood, Washington
The Prudential Insurance Company of America, Newark,
New Jersey

SAFECO Corporation, Seattle, Washington
Seaman's Bank, New York City, New York
Seattle First National Bank, Seattle, Washington
Security Pacific Bank, Los Angeles, California
Simpson Investment Company, Seattle, Washington
Simpson Paper Company, San Francisco, California
Stone Container Corporation, Chicago, Illinois
Swedish Hospital, Seattle, Washington
U.S. News and World Report, Washington, D.C.
Washington University Medical School, St. Louis, Missouri

SELECTED MUSEUM COLLECTIONS

Albright-Knox Art Gallery, Buffalo, New York
American Craft Museum, New York City, New York
American Glass Museum, Millville, New Jersey
Art Gallery of Greater Victoria, Victoria, British Columbia
Australian National Gallery, Canberra, Australia
Brno Glass Museum, Czechoslovakia
Boston Museum of Fine Arts, Boston, Massachusetts
Carnegie Museum of Art, Pittsburgh, Pennsylvania
The Chrysler Museum, Norfolk, Virginia
Cooper-Hewitt Museum, New York City, New York
Corning Museum of Glass, Corning, New York
Crocker Art Museum, Sacramento, California
Currier Gallery of Art, Manchester, New Hampshire
Dallas Museum of Fine Arts, Dallas, Texas
Decordova and Dana Museum, Lincoln, Massachusetts
Denver Art Museum, Denver, Colorado
The Detroit Institute of Arts, Detroit, Michigan
Elvehjem Museum of Art, University of Wisconsin, Madison, Wisconsin
Everson Museum of Art, Syracuse, New York
Fine Arts Museum of the South, Mobile, Alabama
Finnish Glass Museum, Riihimaki, Finalnd
Glasmuseum Frauenau, West Germany
Glasmuseum Wertheim, West Germany
Grand Rapids Museum, Grand Rapids, Michigan
Haaretz Museum, Tel Aviv, Israel
The High Museum of Art, Atlanta, Georgia
Hokkaido Museum of Modern Art, Hokkaido, Japan
Honolulu Academy of Arts, Honolulu, Hawaii
Hunter Museum of Art, Chattanooga, Tennessee
Indianapolis Museum of Art, Indianapolis, Indiana
Israel Museum, Jerusalem
Kestnermuseum, Hannover, West Germany
Krannert Art Museum, Champaign, Illinois
Lannan Foundation, Palm Beach, Florida
Leigh Yawkey Woodson Art Museum, Wausau, Wisconsin
Lobmeyr Museum, Vienna, Austria
Los Angeles County Museum of Art, Los Angeles, California

Lowe Art Museum, Coral Gables, Florida
Lyman Allyn Art Museum, New London, Connecticut
Madison Art Center, Madison, Wisconsin
Metropolitan Museum of Art, New York City, New York
Morris Museum of Arts and Sciences, Morristown,
New Jersey
Musee des Arts Decoratifs, Paris, France
Musee des Arts Decoratifs de la Ville de Lausanne,
Switzerland
Musee des Beaux Arts et de la Ceramique, Rouen, France
Museum Bellerive, Zurich, Switzerland
Museum Boymans-Van Beuningen Rotterdam,
The Netherlands
Museum fer Kunst und Gewerbe, Hamburg, West Germany
Museum of Art, Rhode Island School of Design, Providence,
Rhode Island
Museum of Contemporary Art, Chicago, Illinois
Museum of Glass, Jablonec Nad Nisou, Czechoslovakia
Museum of Modern Art, New York City, New York
Muskegon Museum of Art, Muskegon, Michigan
National Museum, Stockholm, Sweden
National Museum of American History, Smithsonian
Institution, Washington, D.C.
National Museum of Modern Art, Kyoto, Japan
New Orleans Museum of Art, New Orleans, Louisiana
Newport Harbor Art Museum, Newport Beach, California
Parrish Museum of Art, Southampton, New York
Philadelphia Museum of Art, Philadelphia, Pennsylvania
Phoenix Art Museum, Phoenix, Arizona
Queensland Art Gallery, South Brisbane, Australia
Royal Ontario Museum, Toronto, Canada
Renwick Gallery, Smithsonian Institution, Washington, D.C.
St. Louis Art Museum, St. Louis, Missouri
San Francisco Museum of Modern Art, San Francisco,
California
Seattle Art Museum, Seattle, Washington
Smith College Museum of Art, North Hampton Massachusetts
J. B. Speed Art Museum, Louisville, Kentucky
Tacoma Art Museum, Tacoma, Washington
Toledo Museum of Art, Toledo, Ohio
Tucson Museum of Art, Tucson, Arizona
Umeleckoprumyslove Museum, Prague, Czechoslovakia
University Art Museum, Arizona State University, Tempe,
Arizona
University Art Museum, University of California, Berkeley,
California
University of Michigan, Dearborn, Michigan
Utah Museum of Fine Arts, Salt Lake City, Utah
Victoria and Albert Museum, London, England
Wadsworth Atheneum, Hartford, Connecticut
Whatcom Museum of History and Art, Bellingham,
Washington
Yale University Art Gallery, New Haven, Connecticut
Yokohama Museum of Art

COLOPHON

DALE CHIHULY : JAPAN 1990 is published in an edition of 10,000 copies. Photographs are by Roger Schreiber, Ray Charles White and Mike Seidl. This catalogue will accompany an exhibition of work by the artist at Japan Institute of Arts and Crafts, The Azabu Museum of Arts and Crafts, C-2 Gallery, C-Two Network Co., LTD, Tokyo, Japan. Printed and bound by Toppan Printing, Co., Tokyo, Japan, 1990.